The KRISTIN Method

Why You Never Finish Projects and How to Change That

By
Kristin Laus

Dedication

To every knitter who has ever hidden an unfinished project in the bottom of their basket – this is for you. Your hard work deserves to be completed.

Acknowledgments

To my wonderful family Kip, Karen, Katie & Kai, thanks for always wearing the things I've knit you. To Memory, who taught me that starting with a sweater wasn't crazy. To Grandma Renschigai, whose lime-green acrylic yarn and hot-pink aluminum needles sparked a lifelong journey. To my parents who showed me that creativity is an integral part of life. To all the Starlites for being so fun and so full of inspiration. To every knitter who has shared their struggles and triumphs with me at the yarn shop – your stories shaped this method. And to you, the reader, for being brave enough to face your unfinished projects.

Table of Contents

Forward

The Unfinished Story of Every Knitter (And How It Ends)

I have been part of the knitting world for over twenty-five years as a knitter, a teacher and a yarn shop employee. When I started working at a yarn shop seven years ago, I noticed something.

At first, I couldn't quite put my finger on it.

I just knew something was off.

I would watch people walk into the yarn shop, full of excitement about their new project and choosing the perfect materials. The conversations were always the same—visions of sweaters, blankets, heirloom pieces that would one day be passed down.

And then... time would pass.

They would return, sometimes a week later, sometimes a month, but with a different energy.

When I would ask how their project was coming along they'd say:

"I'll get back to it eventually."

"I just got distracted."

"It's somewhere... I think."

Their enthusiasm for the project was gone. In its place? A strange mix of guilt and avoidance.

Sometimes they hadn't even cast on and the yarn was still sitting in the paper bag from the shop.

I knew what was really happening.

Because it wasn't just one person. It was almost everyone.

At knit night, in online communities, inside the shop where I worked—unfinished projects weren't the exception. They were the rule.

And instead of facing the pain of it, we did what humans always do when something hurts too much.

We turned it into a joke.

We gave our unfinished projects a cute name—UFOs (Unfinished Objects)—so we didn't have to call them what they really were: reminders of every time we lost momentum.

We called our mountains of unused yarn a "stash" instead of what they really were—a graveyard of good intentions.

But behind the humor, I saw what was *really* happening.

Customers would only be half joking when they came up to the register with arms full of yarn telling me they didn't want a receipt because they didn't want evidence of what they had just bought.

They didn't want their partners to find out they were "wasting more money" on something they would never finish.

It would stand there amazed when the same customer would come in every single week, spending hundreds of dollars on a sweater's quantity of yarn—yarn I knew, with absolute certainty, would never become a sweater.

I watched them bury themselves under piles of unfinished projects.

As a former counselor, I felt deep sadness. I knew this wasn't just about knitting—it was about self-worth, about avoidance, about something deeper.

As an organizer, I wanted to go home with them right then and there, clean out their project bins, and help them make sense of the mess.

As a knitter, I knew exactly how scattered and guilty a bunch of UFOs and a huge yarn stash made me.

And that's when I realized—this wasn't about discipline. This wasn't about "finding the time."

Something bigger was happening.

Something no one was addressing.

And I needed to figure out what it was.

The people who finished projects? They had a system. A structure. A method that worked.

The people who struggled to complete a project? They weren't just "busy" or "unmotivated." They were overwhelmed.

And without a clear framework to guide them through it, they got stuck in a cycle of starting, stopping, and feeling worse every time.

I knew there had to be a way to bridge that gap.

To take what I knew about organization and how our minds work—and apply it to knitting.

Not just to help people finish projects, but to help them take back their sense of creativity, confidence, and joy.

Because this is bigger than knitting.

It's about finally learning how to see something through.

To bring your ideas into the world instead of leaving them in a drawer.

And that's exactly why I created The KRISTIN Method.

This isn't just another knitting book.

It's a step-by-step guide to finishing—every time.

Because you are not the problem.

You just haven't been given the right tools.

Until now.

Questions for Reflection

These questions are designed to help you dig deeper into your knitting journey, confront your habits and mindset, and transform your approach to finishing projects. Use them to reflect at the end of each section, whether you're writing in your book or thinking through your answers. The goal is not just to read but to engage and grow.

When you think about your unfinished knitting projects, do you feel a twinge of guilt or shame? What does that tell you about how you see yourself as a knitter?

_____

_____

_____

_____

_____

_____

Why do you think you keep starting new projects instead of finishing the ones you've already started? What's driving that choice?

_____

_____

_____

_____

_____

_____

What would it feel like to walk into a yarn shop without the weight of unfinished projects hanging over you? How might that change your relationship with knitting?

_____

_____

_____

_____

_____

_____

Chapter K
Knowing Why You Knit

I still remember pulling up to that tiny yarn shop in Birmingham, Alabama, hesitating in my car. *Is this really the place?* It looked more like a house than a store. There was a sign, though, so I got out and walked to the door. *Do I knock? No... it's a shop. I'll just go in.* I had wanted to learn to knit for years, but having a small daughter finally gave me the incentive I needed: I desperately wanted to knit cute little sweaters for her.

The moment I stepped inside, I felt it. The hum of quiet creativity. The scent of wool. The gentle clatter of needles from a group of women sitting around a dining table. This wasn't just a store; it was something else entirely.

The Shop That Felt Like Home

The women looked up, curious but welcoming. I couldn't help but notice I was decades younger than any of them. It felt like I had stepped into a secret society, one I wasn't sure I belonged to. Then, the woman at the head of the table smiled and said, *"Hi, I'm Memory. Let me know if you need any help."*

And just like that, I was in.

Diving Straight In

I told Memory that I had always wanted to learn to knit, that my grandmother had tried teaching me at seven, but I hadn't had the patience. I mentioned that I wanted to make sweaters for my daughter, but didn't know where to begin.

Memory nodded. *"Then we'll start with a sweater for you."*

Wait—what?

"Shouldn't I begin with a scarf?" I asked, already picturing my inevitable failure.

"Nope. A scarf is boring. You'll give up. A sweater is just two rectangles and two sleeves. It'll be way more interesting. You can do this."

She said it so matter-of-factly that, despite my doubts, I believed her.

Tying the Threads to Family

I picked a teal cotton-blend yarn that felt good in my hands. As I struggled through casting on, my mind drifted to my grandmother and that one time she tried to teach me to knit. I remember the lime-green acrylic yarn on the hot-pink aluminum needles, as I struggled to knit as she sat next to me on the couch crocheting and watching her "stories" on TV. I felt something tighten in my chest. *She would have loved to know I was doing this.*

For the first time, I understood: knitting wasn't just about making things. It was about connecting—to family, to creativity, to something timeless.

The Inner Resolve

The learning curve was steep. My fingers fumbled. The tension was all wrong. Every few stitches, I sighed in frustration.

But then a thought hit me: *Lots of people have learned this. Why not me?*

I straightened my back. Focused. And slowly, stitch by stitch, I began.

Beginning with the Why

Looking back, I see now that knitting is never just about knitting. It's about how we approach learning, struggle, and perseverance. It's about stepping into something without waiting for perfect conditions.

And it's about starting. Because *you can think and think about doing something, but it only counts when you begin.*

Embracing the Journey

When I think about that little gray house, those women at the table, and the way I almost didn't walk through the door, I realize how pivotal that moment was. It was a neon sign from life saying, *Stop waiting. Just start.*

So, I did.

And now, it's your turn.

HINT:

Knitting is never just knitting. And what you do next might just teach you something far greater than stitches.

Questions for Reflection

What first drew you to knitting—beyond just wanting to make something? Dig deep: what need or desire were you hoping it would fill?

_____

_____

_____

_____

_____

_____

Have you ever felt a thread connecting you to someone or something bigger through your knitting—like family, tradition, or even yourself? What did that moment reveal to you?

_____

_____

_____

_____

_____

_____

If you had to define your personal "why" for knitting right now, what would it be? How does that "why" shape the way you approach your projects?

_____

_____

_____

_____

_____

_____

Chapter R
Recognizing Patterns (Beyond the Yarn)

I had been working on a top-down colorwork sweater. The gauge was off, and I had already pulled the yoke all the way out twice. And now, just as I reached the part where the sleeves separated, I realized—again—that it was still too big. All that effort, and I had to start over. Again.

I stared at it, exhausted. *I can't do this right now.* I shoved it down to the bottom of my knitting basket, telling myself I'd come back later. But to be honest, I wasn't sure I would.

Avoiding Pain, Seeking Comfort

That moment—the moment I nearly gave up—wasn't about my ability to knit. It was about my reaction to discomfort. Nearly every decision we make is driven by one of two things: avoiding pain or seeking pleasure. And in that moment, ripping out stitches for the third time felt unbearable.

So, I escaped. I let the frustration win. I left the sweater in the basket, convincing myself it was a temporary break. But deep down, I knew: *If I don't come back to this, it will stay unfinished forever.*

Facing the Reality

A few weeks later, I pulled it out again. I looked at it with fresh eyes and thought, *I can do this. Pulling it out one more time won't kill me.* I ripped it all back (again!), made yet another gauge swatch, cast on once more, and this time, something shifted. The tension evened out, and suddenly, the gauge was right.

That sweater? It fits perfectly. I wear it all the time. And now, when I see it, I don't just see the finished project—I see the process. The frustration, the pause, the return, and the eventual triumph.

Recognizing the Patterns in Your Mind

This wasn't just about knitting. It was a pattern—one I had followed in other areas of my life. The moment something became too frustrating, too tedious, too imperfect, I walked away. Not just from knitting projects, but from jobs, relationships, and opportunities.

When I think about those patterns—like the moment I shoved that top-down sweater into my basket—I realize there's more to uncover. It's not just about frustration or avoidance; it's about how our brains react under pressure and how we can train ourselves to push through with kindness. Let's dive into that in Chapter T: Training Yourself to Finish Without Resistance.

Look at your own unfinished projects. What made you stop? Was it boredom? Frustration? The creeping doubt that you might not be able to do it perfectly?

What if, instead of seeing those feelings as reasons to stop, you saw them as part of the process?

A New Approach to Frustration

Instead of giving in to frustration, what if you adjusted how you approached it? Next time you hit a wall, try one of these shifts:

- **Step away intentionally.** Instead of shoving a project in a drawer out of frustration, decide how long you'll take a break and when you'll return.

- **Change the environment. Knit** somewhere new. Work on a tricky project while sitting in the sun or at a cozy café instead of at your usual spot at home. Take it to work on at your local knitting group.

- **Reframe the struggle. Instead** of saying, *I can't do this,* ask, *What's one thing I can adjust to make this easier?*

Frustration isn't the enemy—it's part of the creative process. The key is learning how to move through it instead of letting it stop you.

Your Next Step

The next time you're tempted to shove a project aside, pause. Ask yourself: *Am I really done with this, or am I just avoiding the discomfort of figuring it out?*

Because if you've unraveled it twice, maybe it's worth unraveling one more time.

Questions for Reflection

What's the most common reason you abandon a knitting project—boredom, frustration, doubt? Can you spot that pattern showing up in other parts of your life?

_____

_____

_____

_____

_____

_____

When you hit a tough spot in a project, do you lean into the challenge or step away from it? What does your choice say about how you handle discomfort?

_____

_____

_____

_____

_____

_____

What would need to shift inside you to see frustration as a signal to keep going instead of a reason to stop?

_____

_____

_____

_____

_____

_____

Chapter I
Intentional Stitches: A Framework for Finishing

Hey, you can keep knitting the way you always have—starting projects, setting them aside, feeling guilty, and wondering why you never finish anything. You can keep repeating that cycle. Or you can take a step back, look at the reality of that frustration, and admit that *it's not working.*

That feeling—the disappointment, the guilt, the weight of unfinished projects—it's too much. It's time to try something different.

The truth? Finishing doesn't have to be complicated. It comes down to just three non-negotiables. And once you see how simple they are, you'll wonder why you weren't doing this all along. So, I invite you in—not to try harder, not to rely on motivation, but to step into a system that actually works.

The Three Non-Negotiables of Finishing

This method isn't based on *motivation*—because motivation is fleeting. It's built on three essential rules that transform knitting from a cycle of unfinished projects into a steady rhythm of completion.

Non-Negotiable #1: Show Up for 20 Minutes a Day

Most people wait for motivation. They think they'll knit on that unfinished project when they *feel like it.* But if you only show up when you're inspired, you'll never finish anything.

The trick? Make the action so small that skipping it feels ridiculous. That's why I start with **20 minutes a day**. Not an hour. Not an entire evening. Just enough to make progress without feeling overwhelmed.

- Too busy? You still have 20 minutes.

- Not in the mood? You still show up for 20 minutes.

- Feeling stuck? Even sitting with your project for 20 minutes counts.

And pay attention to timing. Are you a morning person? Schedule your 20 minutes before noon when your prefrontal cortex (your logical brain) has more power. Night owl? Your best knitting might happen after dinner when your brain is ready for focused work.

This isn't about speed. It's about reinforcing the habit of *continuing.* It's about working with your brain's natural rhythms instead of fighting against them.

Non-Negotiable #2: Find a Community

Knitting *feels* like a solo activity, but isolation is the quickest way to quit. When you struggle alone, it's easy to stop. When you have a group—online or in person—you gain support, accountability, and momentum.

A community does three things:

- **Keeps you grounded** when motivation dips.

- **Provides perspective** when frustration clouds your judgment.

- **Encourages follow**-through when you're tempted to start something new.

Action step: Find a knitting group. Go to your local yarn shop for help. Join our KRISTIN Method SKOOL group. Stop struggling in isolation.

Non-Negotiable #3: Separate Technical Problems from Mental Blocks

When you hit a wall, ask yourself: *Is this a technical issue or a mental block?*

- If you don't know a stitch? **It's a technical problem**. Find a tutorial, ask for help from a friend or at your local yarn shop, or look it up.

- If you feel stuck, frustrated, or doubting yourself? It's a mental block. And no knitting technique will solve it.

Mental blocks require mindset shifts. That's why The KRISTIN Method integrates deeper tools—guided audio, meditations, and structured coaching—to help you break through patterns of avoidance. But for now let's work through what you can with this book.

Your Next Step: Step Into the Framework

If you're tired of unfinished projects, it's time to shift from hoping you'll finish to ensuring you do.

- **Knit for 20 minutes** a day. No negotiations.

- **Find a community**. Don't do this alone.

- **Use the right tool for the right problem**. Don't mistake frustration for failure.

You don't need a new system. You need *this* system.

Now, set your timer for 20 minutes. Pick up your knitting. And begin.

Questions for Reflection

Have you ever committed to knitting for just 20 minutes a day? If not, what's holding you back from trying it now?

_____

_____

_____

_____

_____

Who's in your knitting corner—friends, a group, a community? If you're going it alone, how might connecting with others change your finishing game?

_____

_____

_____

_____

_____

_____

Think of a time you got stuck on a project: was it a complicated pattern (technical) or your own headspace (mental)? How can you tackle those differently next time?

_____

_____

_____

_____

_____

_____

Chapter 5
Simplifying to Create Flow

Let's be honest: it's not just unfinished projects weighing you down—it's the sheer volume of them. The excess yarn. All the favorited Ravelry patterns. The decision fatigue that keeps you paralyzed before you even begin.

You know what it feels like to start something new. That spark of excitement. That rush of possibility. And then, before the project is finished, another pattern catches your eye. Another skein calls your name. Before you know it, your space is cluttered with half-finished projects, and instead of feeling joy, you feel guilt. Frustration. Maybe even shame.

Hey, I see you. You tell yourself it's fine. That you'll come back to those projects *someday*. That you just need the right mood, the right inspiration, the right time. But let's be real—you and I both know that someday rarely comes.

The Illusion of Progress

New projects **feel** productive. The thrill of casting on, the excitement of fresh potential—it tricks you into believing you're making progress. But if you're always starting and rarely finishing, you aren't progressing. You're just chasing the next high.

I watched this happen all the time in the yarn shop. A customer would come in and buy a sweater's worth of yarn. A week later? She'd be back. Still excited—except now she was buying yarn for a *different* sweater. The first one? Already forgotten. Not because she didn't love it, but because something new felt more fun in the moment.

Sound familiar?

If it does, it's time to stop pretending that more projects will make you happier. Because they won't. More choices don't create more joy—they create more distraction. And distraction is the enemy of finishing.

The One-Project Rule (And Why It Works)

Do you look at all your unfinished projects and not know where to start? It might seem obvious, but one of the simplest ways to eliminate decision fatigue is to work on one project at a time.

No more juggling. No more guilt. No more wondering which half-finished sweater deserves your attention today. Just clear, focused progress.

But listen, I get it—some people thrive on variety. If the thought of only working on one project makes you twitch, you don't have to go cold turkey. There's another way.

The Two-Project Balancing Act

For those who need a little variety, I recommend keeping just two active projects:

- **A mindless project** – Something repetitive that you can work on while watching TV, listening to a podcast, or sitting in a meeting.

- **A challenging project** – Something that stretches your skills, keeps you engaged, and pushes you forward.

That's it. Two projects. Enough for variety, but not so many that you feel scattered and overwhelmed.

Still feeling weighed down? Then it's time for project triage.

The Project Triage Method

If you've got a bunch of unfinished projects sitting around, it's time to get brutally honest. Let's sort them into three categories:

1. **Finish Now** – The projects you *still love*, that excite you, or are already close to completion.

2. **Pause for Later** – Projects you still want to finish but don't need to work on right now.

3. **Let Go** – Projects that no longer serve you. The ones you're holding onto out of guilt, not genuine excitement.

Start with "Finish Now." Pick one and commit to it. If multiple projects fit, prioritize based on which one feels the most exciting or is closest to done.

Put away the "Pause for Later" projects. Get them out of sight. They're not your focus right now.

Release the "Let Go" projects. Be honest—if a project has been sitting untouched for years, do you really want to finish it? Or are you just holding onto it because you feel like you *should*?

If it no longer excites you, set it free. Someone else will love that yarn. Frog it. Wind the yarn. Donate it. Gift it. Repurpose it.

Letting go isn't failure—it's freedom.

The Joy of Less

Knitting should feel like flow, not like an ever-growing pile of unfinished work that haunts you.

The fewer choices you have, the less mental clutter you carry. The less guilt you feel, the more you can actually knit.

So take a deep breath. Look at your projects and ask yourself:

What would it feel like to be free from this weight?

Then take the first step. Choose one project. Set the others aside. And let yourself finally finish.

Questions for Reflection

How many projects are sitting unfinished in your space right now? Be honest—how does that number make you feel when you look at it?

_____

_____

_____

_____

_____

_____

What happened the last time you tried focusing on just one project—or even two? Did it free you up or freak you out?

_____

_____

_____

_____

_____

_____

If you had to let go of one unfinished project today, which would it be? What's stopping you from releasing it for good?

_____

_____

_____

_____

Chapter T
Training Yourself to Finish Without Resistance

You probably already know this cycle: Excitement. Start. Frustration. Pause. Abandon. Repeat.

That burst of energy when you begin a new project? It's intoxicating. But what happens when the excitement fades? When the rows get tedious? When it stops feeling fun?

For so many knitters, that's the moment of truth. And most don't push through.

So let's be real—right now, you don't have a finishing problem. You have a resistance problem. And if you don't face it, you will stay stuck in the loop forever.

The Heavy Cost of Procrastination

Before we move forward, let's talk about why this matters so much. Chronic procrastination isn't just frustrating—it's heavy. Those piles of unfinished projects aren't just clutter in your basket; they're weighing on your mind and body, like a blanket you love but won't finish. That guilt you feel when you see that half-finished shawl? It's not just emotional—it's physical. But we can break this cycle, and it starts with understanding why your brain stalls—and being kinder to yourself.

Why Your Brain Stalls on Knitting

Your brain isn't lazy—it's protecting you. Research shows we'd rather have people think we "lack effort" than "lack ability." That's why, when you pick up that tricky lace shawl and are afraid you'll mess it up, you might set it aside instead of diving in. I've watched lots of people do this—buying yarn for a gorgeous project, then not casting on because they're scared it won't turn out perfect. It's not about not wanting to knit; it's your brain avoiding discomfort.

This creates a brutal cycle: You put it off to feel better now, but that builds more stress later. Your brain sees the project as even more threatening, so you delay again. It's like hiding that half-finished shawl in your drawer, hoping the guilt will fade—but it doesn't.

The Power of Self-Forgiveness

Here's the first step, and it might surprise you: Self-forgiveness. It sounds gentle, but the data is clear—students who forgave themselves for procrastinating on one exam procrastinated less on the next. For knitters, that means letting go of shame over that sweater you abandoned last month. Don't beat yourself up for stalling; instead, say, "It's okay—I can pick it up now and make progress." That kindness breaks the cycle, stitch by stitch, and frees you to keep going.

Action Beats Thinking—Every Time

Here's the key to breaking through: Researchers found that chronic procrastinators share one habit—they try to fix the problem by thinking about it. They analyze why they stall, plan to start, or beat themselves up over it. But studies show action and focus beat thinking, every time. Even just five minutes of knitting—picking up your needles, knitting just a row, or even just a few stitches—can rewire your brain's threat response. It's like telling your emotional brain, "Hey, this isn't scary—it's just knitting."

Think about that half-finished shawl you've been avoiding. Instead of overthinking, work on it for five minutes today. That small action can break the cycle, stitch by stitch. Just start without hesitation, like ripping off a band-aid, and let action—not guilt—move you forward.

With this understanding and kindness, you're ready to build a habit of finishing.

The Shift From Trying to Being

Most people approach finishing as a task. A thing they *should* do.

But here's the thing: A finisher isn't someone who forces themselves to finish. A finisher is just... someone who finishes.

It's not about trying harder. It's about shifting into a new identity— one where quitting isn't an option because finishing is just *who you are.*

Right now, you might be thinking: *But I'm just not wired that way. I've never been someone who finishes things.*

That's fine. Neither was I.

The Truth About Resistance

Here's what I've learned: Resistance isn't about difficulty. It's about discomfort.

- You hit a confusing part of the pattern? Your brain says, "I don't know what to do next."

- The project isn't as fun anymore? Your brain says, "This part is boring."

- You feel stuck or frustrated? Your brain says, "I should just start something else."

Your brain isn't sabotaging you on purpose. It's just wired to avoid discomfort. But the problem is, avoidance doesn't make the discomfort go away—it just delays it.

That's why you need a strategy for handling resistance when it shows up.

The Five-Minute Rule

The next time you feel the urge to set a project aside, commit to five more minutes.

That's it. Just five minutes. Not because five minutes will finish it, but because five minutes shifts your brain out of avoidance and back into action.

This works because of how your brain processes tasks. When you feel resistant to a project, your limbic system (the emotional part of your brain) is essentially winning a tug-of-war with your prefrontal cortex (the logical part). The limbic system screams "This is uncomfortable! Do something else!" while your prefrontal cortex whispers "But we should really finish this."

Five minutes is short enough that your limbic system doesn't panic, but long enough that your prefrontal cortex gets a foothold. It's the perfect compromise.

And here's the beautiful part: Once you're past those first five minutes, continuing becomes dramatically easier. Your brain stops treating the task as a threat and starts treating it as something familiar.

Momentum beats motivation. Every single time.

Your Brain Loves a Fresh Start (Use It Wisely)

Starting a new project feels amazing because it gives you instant momentum. The yarn is new, the idea is exciting, and your brain lights up with possibility.

But the thing is, you don't actually need a new project to get that rush. You just need to shift your focus on the one in front of you.

Try this: Next time you're bored with a project, change one small thing about how you work on it.

- Knit in a different chair.

- Work in a different room.

- Listen to something new/watch a new show

- Set a timer and challenge yourself to knit without stopping for 20 minutes.

Small changes trick your brain into feeling like you're doing something new—without abandoning the project in front of you.

Stop Negotiating With Yourself

The biggest mistake people make? They treat completion as optional.

They let their mood decide. They wait until they feel like it.

But if you only knit when it's easy, you'll never finish at all.

A finisher doesn't sit around wondering *if* they'll keep going. They just keep going.

You don't have to feel inspired. You just have to decide.

Your Next Step: Finish Something Small— Now

This isn't about willpower. It's about momentum. So here's your challenge: Go through your UFOs and finish something small today.

- A dishcloth that's half done.

- A simple hat that only needs a few more rounds.

- That project you abandoned just before binding off.

Whatever it is, finish it. Today.

Why? Because the fastest way to become a finisher is to finish something.

And once you do? The next finish will be even easier.

So stop overthinking it. Pick up your project. And finish.

Questions for Reflection

When resistance creeps in—like boredom or fear of messing up— what does it feel like in your body and mind? How do you usually respond?

_____

_____

_____

_____

How do you talk to yourself when you procrastinate on a project? Could a little self-forgiveness change how you pick up those needles again?

_____

_____

_____

_____

_____

What would finishing a project without that inner tug-of-war mean to you? How might that shift ripple into the rest of your life?

_____

_____

_____

_____

_____

_____

Chapter I
Integrating Knitting into Your Life

You already know the cycle: Knitting in bursts. Stopping for days, weeks, maybe months. Feeling guilty every time you see that half-finished project in the corner.

You tell yourself you'll get back to it. That you just need to be in the right mood, find the right time. But the right time never comes.

Let's stop pretending this is about time. It's about integration.

If you want knitting to be part of your life—if you want to finish things consistently—you can't treat it as something you do *when everything aligns perfectly*. You have to make it *so natural, so automatic* that it becomes just another part of your day.

And remember this crucial truth from the research: procrastination isn't about being lazy. It's about how your brain processes challenges, especially when you're tired, stressed, or overwhelmed. So beating it isn't about being "better" or trying harder—it's about being kinder to yourself and setting up systems that work with your brain, not against it.

Knitting Becomes Natural Through Habit, Not Willpower

Some people think finishing is about discipline. It's not.

It's about designing your day so that knitting isn't something you "squeeze in" but something that naturally happens.

Ask yourself: What do you already do every single day?

- Do you make coffee in the morning?

- Do you watch TV at night?

- Do you sit through meetings, scroll your phone, or listen to podcasts?

What if knitting just *fit* into one of those moments? No debate. No deciding. Just automatic.

Timing Your Knitting for Success

Your logical brain works best when you're not tired, stressed, or overwhelmed. If you're a morning person, block off 20 minutes before 2 p.m. to pick up your needles—maybe during your coffee or breakfast routine, while the house is quiet and your mind is sharp.

If you're a night owl, save that time for after 4 p.m., when the day's chaos settles and you're ready to focus on those stitches. I've seen knitters transform their progress by scheduling knitting during their peak energy—finishing projects they'd abandoned for months.

Kindness Keeps You Going

Integrating knitting isn't just about timing—it's about kindness. Forgive yourself for those unfinished projects in your basket. Don't let shame hold you back from picking up your needles. I've watched knitters carry guilt like a heavy skein of wool, but when they let go of that weight, they found joy in knitting again.

Tell yourself, "It's okay I paused that shawl—I'll pick it up today with fresh eyes." That kindness opens the door to consistency.

Portable Projects: Knitting That Fits Into Your Life

If you only work on massive, complex projects that require a whole setup, you're making it too hard on yourself.

Make it easy. Have a portable project.

A small sock, a hat, a scarf—something that can live in your bag.

Something you can pick up anywhere, without needing a dedicated knitting session.

Something that turns "wasted" moments into progress.

Think about it: How many minutes a day do you lose to mindless scrolling? To zoning out?

What if, instead, you knit a few stitches?

The Truth About Stopping and Starting

If you keep stopping and starting, let me be blunt: you probably won't get out of that cycle alone.

There are endless reasons why someone struggles to stay consistent—lack of time, frustration with a project, having trouble with a new technique. But the real problem?

You haven't built a system that makes knitting the obvious choice.

And systems always win over willpower.

The Fastest Way to Stay Consistent? Find a Group

You think you need more discipline. You don't. You need people.

A knitting night at your local yarn shop.

An online knitting group.

A structured cohort where people actually finish things together.

If you've struggled with finishing in the past, ask yourself: Have I ever had real accountability?

Because when you have people checking in, encouraging you, expecting you to keep going—you do.

Before you tell yourself that maybe you're just not a consistent knitter, ask yourself:

Do I actually dislike knitting? Or am I just frustrated by my own inconsistency?

Have I set up my life in a way that makes knitting easy and natural?

Am I trying to do this alone when I'd actually thrive with others?

Because if knitting is something you love, if it does bring you joy when you actually do it, then the problem isn't knitting. The problem is structure.

Your Next Step: Make Knitting Automatic

Pick a trigger. Attach knitting to something you already do every day (morning coffee, TV time, waiting in the car).

Start small, like we've said before. Commit to two rows/rounds. Or five minutes. A tiny bit is better than nothing.

Find your people. Whether it's a local group, an online community, or a structured accountability space—stop doing this alone.

Look at your schedule. When are you most alert—morning or evening? Block off 20 minutes there, starting with five minutes if that feels easier. Be kind to yourself about past projects, and lean on our community for support. That's how you weave knitting into your life, stitch by stitch, until you're not just a knitter but someone who finishes projects.

Knitting isn't just something you do. It's part of who you are.

Now, make your daily life reflect that.

Questions for Reflection

How often does knitting show up in your week—daily, randomly, or barely? What's one small way you could weave it into your routine starting today?

_____

_____

_____

_____

_____

_____

What's a tiny knitting commitment you could stick to—like two rounds/rows a day? Why does making it small feel hard or easy for you?

_____

_____

_____

_____

_____

_____

Have you ever knit with others and felt the difference? If not, what's keeping you from finding your people?

_____

_____

_____

_____

_____

_____

Chapter N

New Identity: Becoming a Finisher

You've come a long way. This is the payoff. There is nothing more for you to DO.

You started with a ton of unfinished projects—shawls, sweaters, scarves that started off with a bang but never saw the light of day. You faced the resistance, learned to recognize the patterns, knitted with intention, simplified your approach, trained yourself to push through, and integrated knitting into your life with kindness and action.

Now, it's time to step into a new identity: someone who finishes. Not someone who abandons projects, but someone who sees them through—row by row, stitch by stitch. You're not "the knitter who never finishes" anymore. You're the knitter who completes cowls for friends, finishes sweaters for family, and shares finished projects with pride at knitting group or the yarn shop.

This identity isn't built overnight. It's woven through small actions— 20 minutes a day, five minutes to start, forgiveness for past stalls, and community support. It's about knowing when your brain is ready, casting on without hesitation, and letting kindness guide you.

There's nothing quite like the feeling of completing something you've poured time, skill, and creativity into. The moment you bind off that last stitch, block your work, weave in the ends, and hold your finished project in your hands—it's real. It's done.

And then it happens—a quiet exhale of knowing.

You did this. It is finished.

It's not loud. It's not flashy. It's just complete.

But here's the truth: this final chapter isn't just about knitting anymore.

It's about who you are becoming.

A Finisher Sees Things Through

A finisher isn't just someone who gets things done. A finisher is someone who follows through, every time.

They don't wait for motivation. They show up, even when it's inconvenient. They don't make excuses. They find solutions. They don't let frustration stop them. They push through.

This isn't about talent. It's not about discipline. It's a mindset shift.

Right now, you might think, I've never been that person. I always leave things half-done.

Guess what? That was the old you. You're stepping into something new.

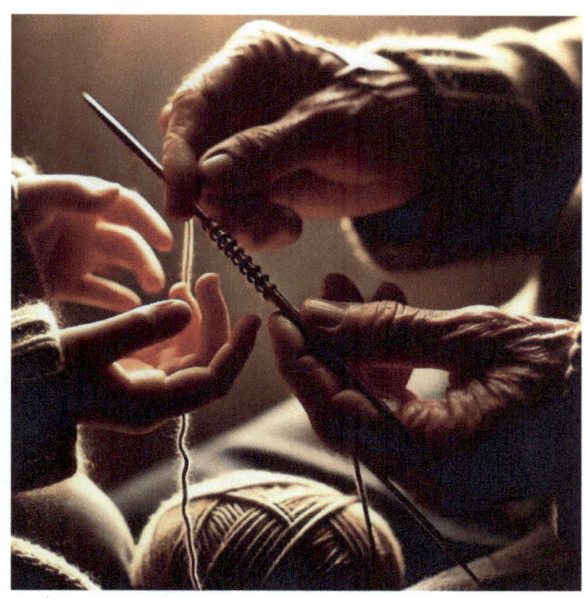

The Payoff: The Joy of Completion

There is a deep satisfaction in finishing a project. When you complete that sweater or pair of socks, you create proof of who you are.

Imagine gifting a handmade shawl to a loved one, watching their face light up as they run their fingers over something you crafted with care. Imagine pulling on a sweater that fits perfectly—because you made it, stitch by stitch, without giving up. Imagine looking in your sweater drawer and seeing finished projects, not just abandoned ideas.

Finishing isn't just about you. It creates joy that ripples outward in the gifts you give and in the pride you have when you wear something beautiful you made with your own two hands.

When you finish something and gift it, you're offering a part of yourself. When you finish something and wear it, you're carrying a tangible reminder of your ability to follow through. When you finish a project and pass on your artwork, you're linking yourself to generations of knitters who came before and those who will come after.

Think of it like this: every project you finish adds to your legacy. Your project will be around long after you leave this earth.

The Identity Shift: You Are a Finisher

This is the final step: fully stepping into your identity as someone who finishes what they start.

A finisher doesn't sit around wondering if they'll complete something. They just do. A finisher doesn't let self-doubt win. They take action anyway. A finisher doesn't wait for permission. They decide.

You are not just someone who starts things. You are someone who sees them through.

Questions for Reflection

Do you see yourself as someone who finishes yet, or are you still stuck in the "starter" mindset? What's the biggest thing holding you back from claiming that new identity?

_____

_____

_____

_____

_____

_____

Picture finishing that one project you've been dodging forever— what would that victory feel like, and who would you share it with?

_____

_____

_____

_____

_____

_____

How could calling yourself a finisher change not just your knitting,
but how you show up in other corners of your life?

_____

_____

_____

_____

_____

Afterword with An Invitation, Not a Push

If this book has resonated with you, then you already know— knitting is more than just yarn and needles. It's about how we engage with creativity, with ourselves, and with time itself.

And if you want more—more guidance, more community, more completed projects—those doors are open.

Join my finishing focused knitting community on the SKOOL platform (skool.com/thekristinmethod) where we have weekly meetings to support each other in finishing projects. There are tons of my videos that guide you through the transformation to being someone who finishes projects. We have a library full of guided knitting meditation resources to turn frustration into flow. Be part of our online community, where we all share our progress, growth, and completed projects.

And now this brings us to a close, my knitting friend. It is my sincere hope that this book has helped you to understand your knitting life and has given you practical solutions on setting yourself free. If you join our community I'm sure we will connect and if not I wish you the very best in transforming yourself and putting those completed knits into the world!

Connect with The KRISTIN Method:

Website: www.thekristinmethod.com

Instagram: @thekristinmethod

YouTube: https://www.youtube.com/@TheKRISTINmethod

SKOOL: https://www.skool.com/thekristinmethod

TikTok: @thekristinmethod

Email: kristin@thekristinmethod.com

About the Author

Kristin has spent over twenty-five years in the knitting world as a knitter, teacher, and yarn shop employee. With a Master's Degree in counseling, she brings a unique perspective to the challenges faced by knitters everywhere. Her method combines psychological insight with practical strategies to help knitters not just start, but finish their projects.

Through her work at an independent yarn shop and her online presence, she has helped hundreds of knitters transform their relationship with their craft. The KRISTIN Method emerged from years of observing patterns in how people approach their projects and developing systematic solutions to common obstacles.

When she's not exploring, teaching, or traveling, you can find her working on her latest knitting project: an insanely detailed anatomically accurate fruit bat.

To learn more, please visit: thekristinmethod.com

www.ingramcontent.com/pod-product-compliance
Lightning Source LLC
Chambersburg PA
CBHW040848120626
46547CB00001B/83